Some Naval

CW00670872

Mordaunt Hall

Alpha Editions

This edition published in 2023

ISBN : 9789357961455

Design and Setting By
Alpha Editions
www.alphaedis.com
Email - info@alphaedis.com

Contents

PREFACE

A BOOK containing accounts of the work continually and unceasingly being carried on by the gallant officers and men of the Royal Navy should prove of considerable interest to all, and, at the present time, especially to the American reader. I am glad that a New York journalist has had the opportunity of witnessing a part of the titanic task of our courageous sea-fighters, and of personally gaining an idea of the hardships endured by the plucky men who are watching our coast. This little book may help considerably to enlighten the general public on the work of the branches of the Navy, and prove that the men engaged in this tedious, hazardous, and nerve-racking vigil are going about it with the same old valour befitting the traditions of the Royal Navy. They have fought the savage beasts like true sportsmen. They have rescued enemy sailors, clothed and fed them, without a sign of animus, knowing that victory will crown their efforts to throttle the enemy of humanity and of civilisation. And that enemy is now the common foe of the United States as well as of England. He has been the sly enemy of the United States even before the declaration of hostilities by the American Congress, while he was the avowed enemy of other countries engaged in this terrible war.

These stories, light though they be, give a conception of what it is to search the seas in a submarine, and the bravery of the youngest branch of the Navy—the Royal Naval Air Service—is palpable even from the modest accounts given by these seaplane pilots. They have confidence in their supremacy over the enemy, and are all smiles even in the face of imminent danger. It shows that often British coolness and pluck have saved a machine as well as the lives of men.

Of special interest is the talk with the captain of a mine-sweeper while he is on the bridge of his vessel. He tells of the many neutral lives that have been saved by English seamen at the risk of their own vessels and the lives of their crews. Noteworthy is it that Great Britain in the course of this war has not been the cause of the loss of a single neutral life. Mines have been placed at random by Germany's pirate craft.

The grit of the English seaman comes to light in the author's journey in a naval ambulance train, as does also the fact that the service takes the utmost care of its wounded and sick. In the account of the Royal Naval Division it is touching to note that the men who are fighting in France and who distinguished themselves so valiantly in the Ancre and other battles, still cling to sea terms or talk.

The accounts in this volume may cause the people of my native country to appreciate the necessity for silence on the part of the British Admiralty, as now that their ships are linked with ours in the effort to defeat a common enemy the same idea of giving no information to the enemy even at the cost of criticism undoubtedly will be included in orders. Nevertheless, while playing the trump of silence, it is encouraging to read stories of the Navy so that the readers have certain knowledge that silence and brief reports do not mean that nothing is being accomplished. We have recently had an instance of the efficiency and courage of the officers and men in the fight between two British destroyers and half a dozen of the enemy craft, in which the Germans lost two vessels and the British none. Commanders and others greatly distinguished themselves in this conflict, which occurred in the dead of a moonless night. And the deeds of the Royal Navy are certain to be emulated by the officers and men of the United States Navy, for blood will tell.

ETHEL BEATTY.

I. THE LOG OF A NAVAL AIRMAN

MEN of the British services are exasperatingly modest. You are forced to wring stories of experiences from them, and when you are thrilled to the core over their yarns they coolly inform you that their names must not appear. Fortunately, there is something about a story which "rings true." From one of the soundest pilots of the Royal Naval Air Service I heard his experience of the previous day. We will call him "Q," as he happens to be known in the station. It is his middle initial. He is a tall, well-built man of thirty, who knows a seaplane backwards, and it has been woe to the enemy when he met him.

"We started at dawn," he began. "There's not much flying in the dark, only occasionally. First, we ran the machine out of the hangar, and, as usual, tried the engines. In the fading darkness or growing light it is a great sight to see the flames flashing from the exhaust. In the beginning you run your engines slowly. Yesterday one of them kicked a bit. The cause for the hitch was discovered, and they were once more started. Remember that it is expedient that the engines be thoroughly tested before a flight, as you may spend anxious hours if something goes wrong. The spluttering ended, and we ran them up to full speed. This done, we waited for more light before hauling the machine down to the water. Once the seaplane was water-born, we taxied ourselves across the port at moderate speed. As we rose in the air we had to be careful of the masts of the ships in the harbour, especially as it was foggy. We then opened up the engines, and the seaplane rose. It was very thick, so we kept 300 feet above the water, flying on a course. There were two pilots and an observer in the machine. Our next work was to estimate the velocity of the wind. This is always rather difficult, and, at the same time, it is most important to have an accurate estimate of the wind. We steered ahead, hoping to see a mark which would guide the observer in his course; but because of the fog, we were not able to pick up our mark. Hence we had to go on and hope for the best.

"We flew higher, about 1,500 feet, and the clouds were about 800 feet, so we were far above them. For two and a half hours we steered straight ahead on the lonely fog-covered sea. We were to meet some warships which expected us. But even after covering all that distance, we saw nothing at all, and therefore resolved to descend and see what prospects there were of 'landing' and saving our engines. The sea always appears calm to the man flying above it; and even when we were 30 feet only above the water we could not tell whether or no it would be dangerous to the machine to 'land.'

"By that time we were naturally anxious, as we thought that in steering straight ahead, as we had done, we ought to have reached the ships with which we had the rendezvous. So far as we could, with the roar of the wind and the propeller, we held a consultation—nothing verbose—in mid-air to determine what would be the best move. We decided to alter our course so as to be sure of getting in sight of land. Half an hour later we saw the first sign of life since we had been out—an old tramp steamship. Ten minutes after we sighted land. When you are flying at sea the land, especially when it is low-lying, takes you by surprise; it suddenly looms up when you least expect it.

"We then picked up a mark and set off on our course for the rendezvous. So dense was the mist that we could not see more than one and a half miles ahead. However, we raced along at 70 knots on our new course, and in twenty minutes came in sight of the flotilla of warships spread out below in fan-like form, but all moving fast. These ships, you see, keep on the move; but they stay for the time being near the point selected for the meeting. Instructions were signalled to us, and we came up, and flew nearer and nearer the water.

"'Can we land?' was our first question. 'Land' is always used by a seaplane pilot even if there is no land within a hundred miles of him. Our aerial had been thrown out. It was too rough to go on the water—or, at least, not worth risking damage to the seaplane. We carried on our conversation partly by shouting and partly by signals, which were quickly understood. From the ships we received further instructions, and sped on to carry them out. We had no further difficulties, and reached home just before sunset."

As an illustration of modern warfare, and the fact that single British flyers are feared even by two of the enemy's planes, here is a story told by a young Englishman, who knows no nerves when he is in the air, no matter how near he comes to being snuffed out by the shrapnel and bullets. He is a man of 5 feet 10 inches, with clear blue eyes and blond hair—one of those truth-loving Britishers who prefers to err against himself in his reports rather than tell of an uncertainty as a certainty.

"'Saw and attacked a German submarine, which dived before we could close in on her,'" read this man from a log-book. He turned the pages, and a little afterwards came on this:—

"'Sighted German patrol, and exchanged fire. Got over Zeebrugge——'

"That reminds me," he said, looking up from the little book which held the notes of so many exciting events. "They sent me out then when I ought to have been off duty."

He smiled, as did his hearers.

"Well, I got over the Mohl," he added. "That's the German pier at Zeebrugge. The Mohl showed up black, and the water looked lighter in the darkness. I was up about 2,500 feet, and dropped bombs on the seaplane base. I mean, of course, the German air base. Only a few moments, and they showed that they were ready for me, as the heavens around were lighted up with searchlights. I dropped a few more of my 'eggs,' and could not be certain of what damage I accomplished, although I saw flames spurt up from several places. Then the enemy sent up two long rows of rockets, making an avenue of light so that I could have read by it. These infernal things parachute when they get to a certain height and, with the fire hanging from them, stay stationary, leaving but one exit. If I had run the machine into the rockets it would have been ablaze in no time. These fireworks stay in the air for about two minutes, which is a devil of a long time when you are up there. Thanks to this lighted avenue, I showed up more distinctly than I would have done in the daytime. The end of the avenue, I knew, was the target of their anti-aircraft gunnery. I flew out, and shrapnel tore all around me. My machine was struck several times, and, as bad luck would have it, the patent point of my magneto fell out just when I got to the spot where shrapnel was thickest.

"My chances of getting home then seemed pretty slim—engines out of order, lit up by fireworks, up 2,500 feet, and a target clear as a pikestaff for the gunnery. However, I managed to slide in the direction of the ship on the French coast. It seems easy to keep out of the way of the guns; but, of course, they have a demoralising effect on a man in the air. Not so much at dark as in the day, though. Well, I got home all right.

"Only a day or so afterwards I dropped a bomb on or near a German U-boat, and I can't say to this day whether I struck or damaged her.

"'Very lonely,'" murmured the pilot, reading from his log. "'Just saw a torpedo boat.' On the next day, let's see.... Oh, yes.... 'Saw two German destroyers, and raced back to our ship, and British ships sped after the Germans.'

"A day or so later I had run in with two German machines. It chanced that there was a wind blowing about 30 knots, and I was merely out scouting, and did not carry a gun. The two enemy ships were joined by a third, and then they gained sufficient courage to come a bit close. They shot away my aileron control, and we were in a very bad way. For twenty minutes we were continually under fire, and below there was a heavy swell. It really was only through knowing how scared is the enemy flyer when you go for him that I am here to-night. I let the enemy planes get nearer and nearer to me, and by the time they were ready for firing I dived at one of them. This so upset the poise of the three machines that they turned tail and swung around to come at me. They made huge circles to get on my flanks again. All this took time, and during it I was getting nearer and nearer my base. Now and again the enemy machines were like too many cooks and the broth; they nearly crashed into each other. This also upset their nerves. Incidentally, when you are in the air, only the other machine appears to be moving, and you seem perfectly still. My escape is due in part to the arrival of one of our fighting seaplanes. A German is desperately afraid of them, unless there are four Germans to one Britisher. When they saw this fighting Britisher coming they did not take long to get away. They knew who the flyer was, too, for a man's style in the air is always characteristic. They had heard of this flyer before. So they turned tail, and I got back with a machine out of order. 'The Prussian code of politeness,' we call it when they retire with two or three machines against one of ours. It is the respect that they show for our fighting seaplanes. Of course, this does not detract from the confidence we have in our superiority."

I heard also that seaplanes have been called upon to serve at all sorts of tasks on the dismal briny. On one occasion a senior naval officer of an English port received word that neutrals were out in boats, and that they had no water or food. Their steamship had been torpedoed, and their last message by wireless had been caught by the British. The naval officer despatched a seaplane with bread and water, and the pilot delivered it, with other trifling necessities.

One of the most beautiful sights that meets the eye of a seaplane pilot is when he comes on the scouting parties of British warships. They are never at a standstill, and to keep moving and in the same place they all make a wonderful circle at full speed, with one vessel in the centre. That ship is to receive the message or whatever is brought by the seaplane, which in the event of calm weather lands on the water and sometimes sends off one of her officers to talk to those aboard the vessel protected by the ring of speeding grey warcraft.

II. OVER THE NORTH SEA IN A SEAPLANE

TO have an accurate conception of some of the experiences of a seaplane pilot of the Royal Naval Air Service, I took advantage of an opportunity to go aloft over the North Sea.

"Come with me, and we'll get you togged out for the ride," said the gunnery lieutenant. He was a Canadian, who had lived many years in Rochester, N. Y., and it was he who remembered that I would need something warmer than the clothes I wore.

In the room to which he conducted me were many different styles of air garb. He picked down a hat and coat of black leather, observing that they would serve the purpose.

The morning sun shed a yellowish glow on the dancing sea, and the wind was blowing at the rate of 32 knots. It was agreed by all that there would be an excellent view from the aircraft as the day was clear. By the time the gunnery lieutenant and I reached the ways on which the great seaplane rested, men in overalls, begrimed with oil and dirt, were testing the engine. As the great propeller spun round, coats ballooned out with the rush of air, and the noise was such that one could hardly hear one's own efforts to shout. It was a sound which filled you with awe. The propeller was stopped after a few minutes, and the mechanicians shot up the sides of the craft, and punched oil and gasolene into the places where it was needed. Young officers in naval uniforms stood around the machine—all are usually interested in a departing seaplane. Not far from us were many immense sheds in which were some of the newest types of England's youngest branch of the Navy. There were aircraft there which bespoke the inventive genius of the Briton, and the confidence of the young pilots inspired you with pleasure—it was a confidence that they could beat the enemy at one to two.

Presently the chief mechanician announced to the pilot that all was well, and the man who was to take me above the North Sea, attired in his uniform and a thick white woollen scarf, climbed up the seaplane's port side. He signalled to me to follow, showing the places for me to put my feet. The climb was more difficult than I had imagined, and a literal *faux pas* might not have aided the flying ability of the machine.

There was no lashing the passenger to a seat in the plane. The place in which I sat would not have cramped three men, the pilot being in front. There was a loose leather seat cover atop a wooden box as the only sign of comfort.

"Make the best of it," said the pilot. With that, he turned on a switch, and the propeller whirred a warning of departure to the clouds. It was a parting shot to ascertain that the engines were in trim, and after the engine had been stopped the craft was wheeled out into the waters of the bay, and then again the propeller rent the air with a burring noise which is surprising even if you are more or less prepared for it.

For the first few seconds we apparently swung along on the water's surface, then skimmed along, the floats at the sides of the plane bobbing on the slightly crested sea. It was only a matter of less than a minute before I realised that we were rising in the air between sky and water, and with amazing speed we soared, and soon were 300 feet in the air. Still our aircraft climbed and climbed. The ocean, which had been beating on the sands now outside, seemed peaceful and green. The town which I thought had such winding streets when I walked through them now looked as if it had been laid out by a landscape architect. Up, up we travelled, and the higher we were the more deceptive was the North Sea.

Through, or, at least, far above, the opening to the port the pilot steered the seaplane, and far down in the sea I saw a strip of dusky something pushing a white speck before it. The pilot signalled for me to look down. It was then that I realised that this funny little thing was a British submarine going out to sea. The pilot bellowed something; but I could only see that he was shouting, no sound coming to me above the din of the propeller. We steered straight out to sea, and miles away I saw a grey speck—a warship prowling over the lonely depths.

After listening to stories of pilots who have been tossed on the bosom of the waters for twenty and thirty hours, the thought of the hardships these pilots have to undergo came vividly to me. I thought of how I might feel if a dozen anti-aircraft guns made us their target. Behind us the town now had almost disappeared. The officer kept the nose of his machine towards France, and I thought, as we sped on, of the young officer who had an appointment for dinner with his fiancée, and who had descended in the wrong territory only a week before. These daring pilots, however, think nothing of cutting through the air from England to France and taking a bomb or so with them for Zeebrugge on the way.

I began to think a great deal of my pilot. He was about twenty-seven years old, and was cool and certain. He was a dare-devil, and had only been over in England a short time after spending months on the coast near the front.

The town had disappeared, and it was evident that we were practically at the mercy of the compass. I felt no dizziness at the great height. In fact, I had no conception of the altitude of the seaplane then. Perhaps I was comforted by the whirring of the propeller, the thundering rumble of which was increased by the stiff wind. I looked headlong down, and experienced no sensation of fear. I seemed to be in a solid moving thing as stable as a machine on earth or water. We must have been up 4,000 feet and possibly 100 miles out at sea. There was a sameness about the travelling. You heard the roaring blades, and saw the deceitful sea and clouds on a line with you here and there. The pilot turned the plane, and soon we were headed for land. We kept at the same altitude, and after a while beheld the shore line. The marvellous speed of the aircraft appealed to me then, as it was not long before we were over the harbour gates. At the same time, the seaplane just then did not seem to be making any headway. From a height of 4,000 feet the great vessels looked like fair-sized matches. How impossible it seemed to aim straight enough ever to hit one of those narrow things. As we turned around above the town in the direction of the hangars the trembling wings appeared to waver a bit more than usual. I looked down at the town, and we appeared at a standstill. You can tell sometimes when persons are looking at the planes by a speck of white, which is a face. The earth and sea rose nearer, for, as one does not appreciate, the plane was descending.

Our seaplane swung around and around like a bird about to settle, and, as the seagulls do, alighted on the waters against the wind. With remarkable skill and patience the pilot carefully steered the machine until she faced the ways on which waited a throng of air-station officers and waders. Soon we were properly placed, and a dozen men clad in waterproof clothes splashed forward into the water, and caught the floats of the seaplane's wings. As the engine had been stopped before we landed, I got the first chance to speak to my pilot. He told me to get on the back of one of the waders, and in a few minutes I was again on dry land. Then the first thing I thought of was how the machine looked in the air. The officers congratulated my pilot on a remarkably fine landing.

We had been more than two hours and ten minutes in the air, and we were both glad of a good stretch as we walked to the hangar, the burring buzz of the propeller still in my ears.

III. ADVENTURES IN A SEAPLANE

IT was an interesting gathering which faced the warm fire in a smoking-room of an East Coast station of the Royal Naval Air Service. Many of the seaplane pilots who were attired in the blue and gold of naval officers had recently returned from successful endeavours in their hazardous life in the North Sea and on the Belgian Coast. And here they were in old England chatting about their experiences without brag or boast—just telling modestly what had happened.

On one side of the spacious room, on a long, deep leather-cushioned sofa, were an officer of the guards who was known to have an income of at least ten thousand dollars a year, and who had taken to flying for the excitement; a stocky youth of twenty from Salt Lake City, Utah, who was known to have eked out a livelihood on fifty cents a day at Dayton, O., so that he could pay for his training as a pilot; another youngster, scion of a wealthy Argentine family with English connections; and an Englishman, just over thirty, who had been born in California and had heard the 1914 call of the mother country. They were cramped, but comfortable.

In other chairs of the deep, comfy English variety were a rancher from Canada; an Olympic champion, whose name has often figured in big type in New York's evening newspapers; a lieutenant-commander of the Royal Navy, who had hunted big game in three continents; a wind-seared first mate of a British tramp; a tanned tea-planter from Ceylon; a 'Varsity man from Cambridge, whose aim had been a curacy in the English Church; a newspaper man from Rochester, N. Y.; a London broker; the head of a London print and lithographing business, looked upon as one of the best pilots in the service; and a publisher, who in pre-war days had been more interested in "best sellers" than in seaplanes.

All were dreadnoughts who looked upon it as a privilege to give their lives to smash Prussian militarism. If you had asked any one of them for an interview he would have scoffed at the idea. But ordinary newspapermen cannot be blamed for being enthralled at the share of these pilots in the World War. What's printed about them? Just a paragraph to the effect that "Several seaplanes last night bombed Zeebrugge or Cuxhaven." They dashed out into the frigid North Sea with an errand, but their share in the fights and the valuable assistance they have been to Great Britain as scouts are seldom mentioned. Still, they "carry on," asking for no encouragement. And right here it must be explained that "carry on" means to do or die in this war. It is the byword of the British of the day.

It chanced that "Tidy," as we will call him, was the first speaker who had something to say. He had a reason for talking, for some evil genius had followed him for two days. The yarn is best told in his own words, so far as they can be remembered.

"It was my patrol and I started from France at half-past five o'clock in the morning," began the seaplane pilot. "I shot out to sea for about thirty miles, and then continued to run along the coast for about 63 miles. I caught sight of a Dutch ship, and a little while afterwards observed a submarine. Almost as soon as I saw the vessel there was a cloud of smoke. I raced to the scene, knowing then that the Dutch tramp had been torpedoed by a German U-boat. Four miles further on I espied a second submarine. I opened fire on the first submarine, which then I saw had taken in tow a boat evidently containing the survivors of the Dutch vessel. I observed one of the Dutch sailors crawl to the bows of the boat attached to the submarine and cut the rope. At that instant I dropped a bomb, which fell about 25 or 30 feet from the submarine. The under-sea craft went down very quickly, and I descended further and dropped my aerial, and the mechanician-operator sent out a message. I threw other bombs when I thought I detected about where the submarine was in the sea. It was like a hawk after a fish. The other submarine fled without giving me a chance.

"I continued scouting, having warned the British warships that two submarines were in the vicinity. It came over very misty, and in the deep haze I saw three or four German vessels coming out. As I turned, deciding to race home and give the word, my engines failed me. I went down and down, holding off from the white caps of the sea for two and one-quarter hours. My next adventure was the sight of some German aeroplanes. After fiddling around, I got my engine started, and flew up to 1,000 feet above the sea. It was lucky that I started the engine when I did, for the sea was becoming unpleasant. But then my magneto failed me, and I realised what was in store on those wind-torn waters. I was forced to dodge about like a bird with a broken wing. The wind freshened to 40 knots. Although we did our utmost to keep the seaplane off the water, it, of course, had to rest there, and I became horribly seasick. The mechanician and I tried to keep the craft afloat. We fired off our rockets, hoping to attract the attention of a friendly or neutral vessel, but at the same time realising that we might fall victims to the enemy.

"All night the mechanician and I were tossed on the sea without a chance of attracting anyone, as our rockets had given out. The cold was unbearable, and both of us were very seasick.

"Dawn came, and there did not even then seem much more chance of our being rescued than at night time. You could not imagine anything lonelier than a seaplane on the bosom of the North Sea when you are without food or drink. The rocking of the light craft would have made a good sailor keel over with seasickness. The happy moment, however, did come. We were spotted by a mine-sweeper, and she raced to the rescue. Our mangled machine was hoisted on the kite crane of the little vessel. We had been thirty-six hours without food and water, and most of the time bumped about on the sea.

"That would seem to be about enough for the evil genius to perform, eh? But we were doomed to have another surprise in store. I went to bed in a room in a little hotel, and had hardly closed my eyes when there was a great explosion; the whole place seemed about to fall down. I put on an overcoat, and tore outside to discover that those blamed destroyers which I had seen earlier were bombarding the place where I went to sleep. A lucky shot demolished the building next to the one in which I was in bed; then I went back to bed, too tired to care what else happened."

———————————————————————

IV. SWEEPING THE SEAS FOR MINES

THERE are days when a mine-sweeper captain, who is continually running the gauntlet of death, reckons that he has been fortunate. Usually this is when he just escapes being blown to bits with his vessel or sees what can happen to a steamship when it strikes one of the enemy mines planted at random in the North Sea. There are days when he goes out and sees nothing worth while. However, despite the great danger, unseen and unheard until all is over, these mine-sweeper men guide their vessels out daybreak after daybreak, with the same old carefree air, to perform their allotted task in this war.

Many of these men were fishermen, who looked as if they had slipped out of funny stories in their thick jerseys and sou'-westers; now they are part and parcel of the British Navy, proud of the blue uniform and brass buttons and—when they have them—of the wavy gold bands on their sleeves. There are others who were officers and so forth in the mercantile marine in pre-war days. They have sailed the seas from John o' Groats to Tokio: and to them New York is merely a jaunt.

One of the latter, who was a passenger-vessel officer, attracted a deal of attention at an East English port by his indefatigable labour and fearlessness in his risky job, until he was rewarded for more than two years of grinning at death by the Distinguished Service Cross.

He knows Broadway well, can tell you where he likes best to get his hair cut, and where he considers they put up the best cocktail. One day I was permitted to take a trip with this captain-lieutenant—and get back. Mine-sweeping has been written about by persons from Kipling down, so I will just tell you the story as I then saw it.

The skipper stood on the bridge of his dusky-coloured vessel as she soused through the waters of the grim North Sea, his keen eyes ever on the alert fore and aft, and occasionally on the sister ship to his, coupled along with the "broom." They were "carrying on," as usual. This skipper was a man just in his thirties. His face was cheery and round, and body was muscular and thick-set. In spite of the watch he and his first mate kept on this particular occasion, he found time to give me his opinion on certain things interesting to the men who go down to the sea in ships, and also an idea of what it means to be in command of a mine-sweeper.

"You should have been with us on Sunday," he said, as he lighted his cigarette between his cupped hands. "It was more interesting than usual—had something of this damn thrill you talk about ashore and don't know what it is until you've been at the firing front or in one of these blessed ocean brooms. That chap across the way found a mine in his kite, and we had to cut the hawser in double-quick time, and get far enough away from it before we pegged a bullet in one of the horns."

The skipper explained that none of the mines are exploded less than 200 yards from the vessels. He said that the experience he had just related would have sufficed for a day, but that an hour later, when he was still brushing up a part of the North Sea, not far from the coast, he received a warning from a trawler that a mine exposed at low water was just ahead of him. Not in his time had he seen a steamer go astern quicker. Afterwards, they deftly fished around for the mine, snapped its mooring rope, and brought it to the surface. When the mine was at a safe distance from all vessels, a couple of men then aimed their rifles at it until there was a loud explosion which sent sand-coloured water 35 feet and more into the air.

But the affairs of that Sunday were not yet complete. Twenty minutes after the mine had been exploded a great rumble was heard way out at sea, and soon it was ascertained by the captain of the mine-sweeper that a Scandinavian tramp had met her doom by striking a German mine.

"We went off to see if we could pick up some of the poor chaps," observed the skipper. "Among the twenty-one men and boys we rescued were four who'd been passengers aboard a passenger vessel which had been torpedoed by a German U-boat without warning near Malta. They told us, when they got down into our engine-room, that they were just having one hell of a time getting home. I don't blame them for thinking that. Through good fortune, and taking chances of being sent to the bottom ourselves, we have saved the lives of many of these neutrals who might have perished. Yes, here we are mine-sweeping as a job, flying the white ensign of the British Navy; and yet we have found time to save life imperilled by the enemy. Sometimes I wonder what sly Fritz would have to say if he'd even saved a single neutral. He'd be blowing yet. Did you ever stop to think that our Government never has jeopardised a single neutral life? On the other hand, the lives of neutrals that have been rescued at this port run into the thousands. They talk about the freedom of the seas. What else has there been until Germany showed that what she wants is the 'tyranny of the seas.' Leastways, that's how it strikes me. Ever stop to——"

His attention was caught by a signal from the other vessel, and a keen-eyed sailor wig-wagged back an answer. It was all right, although at first I still remembered the timely warning regarding the slightly submerged mine. As a matter of fact, it was merely a desire of the sister ship's captain to turn around and "sweep back," as the land-lubber might term it.

"Let's see," said the commander, "where was I.... Oh, yes.... Realise that we go out and save lives that the enemy imperils far out at sea? They are lives that don't concern us, but we don't feel like letting a poor chap drown if we can help it. On the other hand, our enemy stops at nothing, and, moreover, takes advantage of our humanity. I think that it should be known that we dash out to the rescue never knowing when the ship may go up against one of Fritz's eggs, which may be anywhere in the sea. Why do we go? Just to pick up a benighted lot from an ill-fated tramp, and there's nothing in it. Yet we do it all the time, and the C.O. commends us for it, too."

We came to a new spot in the green sea to sweep. It was fairly rough, and the little vessel bumped and jumped. And this is the work that goes on from daybreak to dusk seven days a week. If a trawler strikes a mine she usually counts on saying good-bye to herself and 80 per cent. of her crew, and the other type of mine-sweeper is lucky if she gets off with a loss of less than 40 per cent.

Back and forth in a monotonous sea we steamed, and you had an idea how dull this work can be sometimes; also that when it comes to sweeping you saw that the North Sea is a big place.

"It's become a science," observed the skipper. "Fritz has a hard time many a night 'laying his eggs,' and the many ways we have of bringing them to the surface has baffled him a good deal."

A torpedo-boat destroyer hove within signalling distance. The commander was handed a message by a sailor. The alert skipper read it, and said:—

"Tell 'em 'yes.'... Just want to know if we had swept around there."

Still the smoke-coloured little vessels kept up the job of plying back and forth in the waters. Men were busy at the stern of the ships watching the wooden kites that are made so as to catch the mines by the hawser that is slung between the two steamers. The slightest sign of a ball-like piece of steel in the sea and the dullness of sweeping is relieved, for then the skipper knows that he has unhooked one of the mines. Along came a submarine, flying the white ensign of the Royal Navy. The mine-sweepers realise that these men have no arm-chair job, and admire the commander and crew of the under-water boats accordingly. A sailor semaphored with his arms, and the commander of the mine-sweeper sent a message back, and the submarine passed slowly on her way.

"If some of those people at home and abroad at their firesides realised what the men at sea have to suffer to keep this coast free they might have a different way of talking," declared the commander, now taking to his much-burned old pipe. "Those chaps that have just come in have had a week without any sleep—or next to none—and their food has all been canned stuff. There are many persons who think the North Sea's a pond—same as they do over in America."

On we steamed in our section of the waters with never a sign of a German mine. Finally, the day came to a close, and the captain ordered the hawser to be slipped and the kite hoisted in the stern crane of his vessel, the like being done by the other sweeper.

As if glad that the day's work was over, the small craft pressed forward to the harbour, and were disappointed to find that a big tramp was taking up the room of their berths. They anchored outside, waiting for the big steamer to get away.

"Do they tell you when you can come alongside the dock?" I asked.

"No need to," said the captain with a smile. "You'll see."

We had been in the open harbour for about twenty minutes when the bows of the ugly vessel came slowly on. An instant later all the small craft were ready to speed to their respective berths in their turns, and it was not so very long before the mine-sweeper was tied to her part of the dock. The commander of the sister vessel to the one I had been aboard came over to us.

"Good ship that of yours?" I said.

"Yes," muttered the man with two rings of the Royal Naval Reserve on his sleeve. "She's all right; but I love this ship. I had her a year ago, and she's a little wonder. It would take me a long while to love another vessel."

My skipper laughed.

"Just one of those days," he said. "Come, let's go and have a spot."

V. THE ROYAL NAVAL DIVISION

BUFFETED about from Antwerp to Gallipoli, Egypt, the Greek Islands, Salonika, and then to France, first under an admiral, then part of an army corps, again under an admiral, and finally back to military regime—the life of the Royal Naval Division, which startled an Empire by their valour on the Ancre, has been one full of thrills, sorrows, threats of extinction, brave deeds, and perilous journeys. They are proud of their naval origin, and are also tenacious of their naval customs, despite the fact that all their fighting has been done ashore and few sailors survive among them.

In August, 1914, Mr. Winston Churchill, then First Lord of the Admiralty, mobilised and organised, as a division for land fighting, reservist seamen, stokers and marines, and naval volunteers whose services were not required afloat, also recruits drawn mainly from among the miners of the North of England and Scotland. Guards' officers, naval and marine instructors— each in his own ritual—help to train them. To the Navy, who raided them when it needed seamen or stokers for its ships, they were "dry-land sailors." To the Army, they were just a bunch of "so-called salts" or "Winston's Own." But their instructors soon recognised that in these grousing, middle-aged stokers, and in these silent stolid illiterate miners and ironworkers from the North Country, they had the raw material of soldiers as fine as Great Britain can breed.

In many respects, the Division has had the worst of both worlds. They have beaten their way steadily to the fore without much recognition in print; but since Beaucourt fell, both military and naval men have been eager to grasp their hands.

Now and again a brief mention fell to their lot while they were in Gallipoli, where the military were attracted to them a bit by the idea of calling their battalions after famous admirals such as Nelson, Drake, Hood, Collingwood, Anson, Howe, Benbow, and Hawke. Sir Ian Hamilton made mention of the fearlessness of the division in his despatches, and Major-General D'Amade eulogised them for their bravery after the frays of the 6th, 7th, and 8th of May, 1915. In June, 1915, the Collingwood battalion was wiped out; of the officers of this battalion and of the Hood, who went to the attack, not one returned unwounded. The other battalions also suffered terribly, having been equally contemptful of danger.

Prior to that they had, of course, been to Antwerp. Even if they did not have a chance to do much, the Division, at any rate, caused the Belgians to hold out for five days longer than they might otherwise have done.

Among the many brave men on the officers' roll are well-known Britishers who have given their lives for their country. There was Rupert Brooke, the poet; Denis Browne, formerly musical critic of *The Times*; F. S. Kelly, holder of the Diamond Sculls record, who also was an exceptionally clever composer and pianist; and Arthur Waldene St. Clair Tisdall, a great scholar and poet of Cambridge. He was awarded the Victoria Cross for his valour on the 25th of April, at Gallipoli, for going to the rescue of wounded men on the beach. To accomplish this, he pushed a boat in front of him. On his second trip he was obliged to ask for help. In all, he made five trips in the face of great danger. He met death in action barely three weeks afterwards.

Lieutenant-Commander Arthur M. Asquith, son of the former British Premier, is one of the gallant men attached to the Hood battalion. He has been through the thick of many fights, and has been wounded more than once, escaping death through sheer good fortune.

And one of the men whom all England was wild about is a New Zealander from Wellington, twenty-seven years old, now an acting lieutenant-colonel, who was described by an eye-witness of the Ancre fighting as "a flying figure in bandages plunging over Germans to Beaucourt." He is B. C. Freyberg, a born soldier and great athlete.

Before the Great War, this marvel of courage was fighting for Pancho Villa in Mexico; and the instant the European conflict started, Freyberg realised that he might do better in Europe. He therefore deserted Villa, and set out afoot for San Francisco. His splendid constitution stood him in good stead, and he arrived there as fit as a fiddle, soon afterwards winning enough money in a swimming race to take him to London. In the English capital he received a commission as a sub-lieutenant in the Royal Naval Division, and his promotion has been rapid.

Colonel Freyberg was caught in a live electric wire in Antwerp; but it was of so high a voltage that he was not killed, sustaining only an injury to his hand and arm. He was even fired at by his own men, who believed that he was a German crawling through the wire. Just before the landing in Gallipoli, on the 25th of April, 1915, it was proposed to throw dust in the eyes of the Turks by landing a platoon at a point on the coast of the Gulf of Saros, where no serious landing was contemplated. To save the sacrifice of a platoon, Freyberg, who was at that time a company-commander in the Hood battalion, pressed to be allowed to achieve the same object single-handed. His wish was granted; and on the night of the 24th-25th of April, oiled and naked, he swam ashore, towing a canvas canoe containing flares and a revolver. He reconnoitred the enemy's trenches, and, under the covering fire of a destroyer, lit his flares at intervals along the beach. He had some difficulty in finding his boat again. A mysterious fin accompanied him during part of the swim. He at first took it to be that of a shark, but found later it belonged to a harmless porpoise. After some two hours in the water, he was picked up, and for this gallant and successful feat he was made a Companion of the Distinguished Service Order. In Gallipoli he was wounded in May, again in July, 1915, and he was mentioned in Sir Charles Monro's despatches in connection with the successful evacuation of the 9th of January, 1916.

Hence, this sailor-soldier in a comparatively short time attracted a good deal of attention among the naval and military authorities; so it was not surprising that when he applied for a permanent commission in the British Army he was given a captaincy in the Queen's Royal West Surrey Regiment. The same day, however, he received this news he was seconded to the Royal Naval Division with the temporary rank of lieutenant-colonel. So he retained command of his old battalion—the Hood.

Inasmuch as the first despatches concerning the storming of Beaucourt referred to Lieutenant-Colonel Freyberg as "a naval colonel," all Britain was wondering who this hero could be. Some of his friends were not long in guessing; but it was not until the next day that Freyberg in name received credit for the remarkable exploit on the north bank of the Ancre. In the first messages of the British success it was set forth that in a battle where every man fought nobly for the honour of his regiment and his country, one individual act of leadership stood out with peculiar distinctness.

A witness of the battle told of the troops on Freyberg's left being held up, and that between him and them ran, roughly parallel with the line of advance, a spur which cut off the effect of the enemy's machine guns. After fourteen hours of fighting, bit by bit, the sea-dog soldiers had plunged through a mile of trenches and ground sorely marked by shells. Three machine guns then were pushed forward well beyond that line, and the still unsatisfied sailor-colonel, his shoulder and right arm swathed in bandages, asked leave to go ahead and attack the village. His men were about 1,000 yards in front of the companies on his left, endeavouring to advance across the northwesterly slope. It was more like a matter of defence than attack. The men were few in numbers, and had fought like tigers for long hours without a rest. However, about 500 men were collected, and the dark of night was spent in organisation. Then, in the misty dawn, some soldier battalions came up to reinforce the left, and onward plunged Freyberg.

Out on the Ancre they say that he got so far ahead of his men that he rubbed his hand over his head and murmured: "Huh—I believe I forgot to tell them to follow me." Whether or not this is true, only Freyberg knows. But we do not remain in doubt as to what he and his men did right afterwards. They ploughed their way through mud and Germans, with the fire of five machine guns peppering them. They stuck right on the heels of the barrage fire, and in less than twenty minutes from that time the Germans had been driven from their stronghold of Beaucourt. Here and there a German post held, and men in the trenches faced the British bombs and cold steel. Still the Teutons soon learned that it was impossible to stop that alarming Briton and his men.

Freyberg formed a semicircular trench around the far side of the new possession, and then they took time to see what had happened to the gallant little band. Freyberg had received his fourth wound, and his brave 500 had dwindled to a number a good deal smaller. The Britishers, somehow, had been unkind in their speed to the Germans, and the enemy was left gaping with wonder at the result of what they at first took to be nothing more than a bit of bluff.

For this remarkable display of valour Freyberg received the Victoria Cross.

Reverting to the division itself, it should be said that every officer of these jolly-jack-tar soldiers has panegyrics galore to cast in the direction of General Sir Archibald Paris, K.C.B., who was in command of the division at Antwerp and the Dardanelles. He lost a leg before the Ancre fighting, and thus was disappointed of being with them for their great success in France. He was succeeded by Major-General Cameron Shute, C.B. What the division has recently accomplished and the way it has terrorised the enemy, like Kipling's "Tyneside Tail Twisters," is a happy thought to General Shute. In one battalion it is estimated that 90 per cent. of the casualties in the Ancre fighting were caused by the closeness with which the sailors clung to the barrage fire. Their grit caused the enemy to pale.

They are pleased and proud of their sea terms, and would not give them up for anything—not even if the soldiers of the King do not fathom their meaning.

It is a case of going to the "galley," while the red-coat that was persists in the "kitchen." The first field dressing-station is nothing but "sick bay" to the R.N.D. man. They "go adrift" when they are missing from parade, and they ask to "go ashore" when they want leave.

VI. A NAVAL SCHOOL

FROM one of several institutions, every six months Britain turns out 2,200 boys who have mastered the elementary rudiments of seamanship and are ready to take their places as ordinary seamen aboard warships. They will not tell you how many of these schools there are in Great Britain alone, but you may learn that no undue activity has been brought about in these places because John Bull is at war. After having waded through the curriculum of these boys, one comes to the conclusion that they are not so far from being able seamen by the time they emerge from this place on the East Coast.

It is especially striking how speedily the youthful mind snatches up the mysteries of signalling and of wireless telegraphy; and one is filled with interest in following the boys from the time they first enter the school to the day they leave.

In a room where they are "kitting up" are twenty or thirty boys who have just arrived. And, as they say in America, there is "no monkey business" about the instructors: either the boys are those who are wanted or they are not. The youngsters receive their first seafaring garb in a large, well-ventilated room. They have been in the bath, and their hair is as close as the clippers can make it. One of them said he was the son of a lawyer; another that his father was in the Royal Navy; a third came of a parson's family; a husky young chap had been a blacksmith's assistant; and another had cooed milk in London streets.

"An'," declared a petty officer, "they all comes here believin' they'll be able to get a pot shot at the Kaiser. Seems to me that they imagine that William is always standing on guard on the rocks of Heligoland, just waiting for them to come along—what?"

In another section of the school the boys are grounded in discipline by a petty officer, and by the time they get through with him they are accustomed to saluting. Follows then a whirl of wonders to them. There is a model of the forepart of a ship, which they can steer, and so learn port from starboard; there is the ingenious manner of dropping a lifeboat into the lap of the sea; and then the interesting work of tying knots, in which the petty officer instructor takes considerable pride.

One of the most interesting rooms of sub-schools is the one where the youthful "salts" are initiated into the mysteries of signalling, where, besides the numerous flags for sea conversation, there is a dummy wireless station, by which they can become proficient operators. They have models of ships, so that they can tell which are British and which are German. Then there are gunnery schools, and it speaks well for the young Briton that 90 per cent. of the pupils have such keen minds that they yearn to learn more of the mysteries of the study of sea fighting; they have the ambition to be really good seamen, engine-room men, wireless operators, or signalmen.

On a section of the school grounds there is a mast on which is hoisted the White Ensign of the British Navy. This spot is known as the quarter-deck, and every time one of the youngsters passes where he can see that mast he salutes reverently. Beyond that there is the recreation ground, where every Saturday afternoon in winter there are half a dozen games of football. The officers help them to enjoy that, too, for, like Americans, they delight in exercise.

It is remarkable what a change a boy undergoes after a few months at the institution. I was told of would-be sailors who were sloppy and dirty when they entered the school being transformed into neat, fine physical specimens.

"A hair-cut, a wash, a change of underwear and other garments makes all the difference in the world," said one of the instructors. "And when you add to this lessons in sea-neatness, a good deal of interesting headwork, manual labour, good food and plenty of recreation, it's no wonder that the mill makes a new boy of one of the seafaring aspirants."

The boys have one great mess-room; and, although they never have been to sea, they are taught to treat the school as if it were a war vessel. They ate with vigour when I saw them, and I was told that the money given to them by the Government is spent for extras in the eating line—principally candies. Each table constitutes a mess, and there are prizes for the cleanest and best-arranged mess; so they arrange their knives, forks, and spoons in a design calculated to catch the prize-awarder's eye. And, incidentally, this idea of giving prizes for the best-kept mess is followed throughout the service.

Each day is started with prayer on the quarter-deck, and an impressive ceremony it is. Honour and glory is what they will tell you they hope to get out of the Navy, and not money. And the idea of honour, as it is known in the Navy, is drummed into them from the moment they enter the school.

To see these youngsters at any meal is to believe that it was the first time they had eaten for a week. They are ravenously hungry, and the food is of such excellence that it makes a visitor feel as if he would like to sit down too. There is little waste here, for I observed that each plate was polished clean; and, when eating was over, the boys bounded out for an hour's recreation on the spacious grounds. On their way many of them paid a visit to the candy-store, and while they were playing they munched candy.

The port where this school is located is a healthful spot, and in war time no person is permitted to board a ferry to the school without a special pass. When you first land you are decidedly struck by the great figure-heads of old war vessels, which are set up on the "quarter-deck" and in front of some of the buildings. There is one of the old Ganges there—a mammoth wooden head of a very black negro. The size of it is startling.

The officers have a charmingly comfortable ward-room and mess-room. In the bay is the second Ganges, now a sort of mother-ship for mine-sweepers and trawlers, and one of the busiest places one can imagine. The King not long ago dined aboard this ship, and is said to have expressed great interest in the work carried on from the Ganges.

VII. "GENTLEMEN, 'THE KING'"

THERE are many traditions to which the Royal Navy still clings, and there are messes afloat and ashore where it is manifest that time has not withered impressive and picturesque features of the days of the wooden warships. For instance, no layman can help being struck by the British naval officers' toast to the King. And the other toasts are offered with such splendid solemnity and grace that it makes one wish that something of the sort could be done at even the minor affairs where civilians are gathered. Of course, the Londoner and the man from Manchester offers his toast at a great banquet, as they do in New York and other American cities to the President of the United States. But although it takes no longer at a naval mess, there is a something about it which places the civilian in the shade. With the Navy it is a mess, and not a dinner where there are many strangers, and every officer has been doing this since he was a boy.

John Bull's naval officers are men who admit the faults of their country. They have travelled, and have seen a good many other countries and peoples. From Osborne and Britannia days sincerity seems to have been inculcated into them. The discipline is inflexible, but kindly. The captain of a "Dreadnought" will take pains to ask a young midshipman to dine with him, and there exists a wonderful thoughtfulness on the part of the officers for the men. British naval officers are lovers of sports, and, having believed the Germans good sports before August, 1914, they cannot condone attacks on non-belligerents or the shooting of nurses. His Majesty's naval officers do great things without talking about them, and at dinner one of the star heroes of the war may be in the next chair to you, but you certainly will not hear it from him.

Opposite me sat a man who had faced death with Scott on the Polar expedition. It was after I had left the mess that I learned this from one of his friends. But at a mess you may hear stories of men who are absent. It was at dinner aboard one of the great, grey sea-fighters that we laughed at the yarn of a young middy, in charge of one of the cutters off Gallipoli when the Turks were sending shells like rain. This midshipman ordered his men to take cover. His men included bearded fellows twice his size and age. They obeyed, as they always obey. Then the youthful fearnought, to show his contempt for danger, stood on one of the cutter's cross-seats, pulled out a cigarette-case almost as large as himself, and puffed rings of smoke skywards.

"I made a jolly fine set of rings that time," he told one of the men.

Another of this tribe was in Cairo on leave when he received word that his ship was to leave sooner than expected. She was in Alexandria. Not having sufficient money to pay his train fare, he requisitioned a motor-bicycle and sped on to Alexandria. From his youthful eyes there welled tears when he was informed that his ship was weighing anchor. Nothing daunted, however, he commandeered a fast motor-boat, and swept out after the warship, which he caught on the go. This is the man who in later years you are apt to meet at the officers' messes—a man full of information and wonderfully versatile. He may have ploughed the seas for many years, and dwelt in his steel home in the baking heat of tropical suns, and waited for the enemy for many a day. Hence conversation never lags at these dinners. The meals are comparatively plain in these days; but most of the officers stick to the delight of a cocktail before dinner, and after the *pièce de résistance* they have their glass of port.

Just before the dessert the port is poured into glistening glasses, and the table is cleared.

"Table cleared, sir," announces the steward to the president of the mess; and a second later one hears: "Wine passed, sir."

"Thank God," is the brief grace of the chaplain; or, if one is not present, the head of the mess says it. This is followed with a rap on the table, and from the president of the mess:—

"Mr. Vice, 'The King.'"

"Gentlemen, 'The King,'" speaks out the vice-president of the mess, who is seated at the other end of the table opposite to the head of the mess.

Conversation, which a second before had been filling the place, is silenced by the grace, and the stranger may be somewhat startled by the suddenness of the proceedings. It is the privilege of these officers to drink the King's health seated. This is an old custom, which came about through the sovereign realising that ships are not the steadiest places always, and the fact that the ward-rooms are sometimes not constructed so that a tall man can always stand erect.

Immediately "Gentlemen, 'The King,'" is uttered by the mess's vice-president each officer repeats in an undertone: "The King." The glasses after being held aloft come to the table as one, and the conversation is resumed. Garbed in their immaculate monkey-jackets, with the glistening gold braid on the cuffs, the men at the carefully set and beflowered table make a scene long to be remembered.

Incidentally, there is a marine officers' mess at a certain port which naval officers are always ready to talk about. In that place they are proud of a wonderful mahogany table which has been polished for many years until it is now like a black mirror. The band of this mess is one of the best in England; and it is the privilege of the bandmaster to play at concerts and in theatres, the proceeds being divided among charities, the bandmaster and his men. Hence the leader of this band probably had an income of $7,500 a year.

Here, before the toast to the King is offered, servants come along each side of the great table and, at a given word, whisk the tablecloth from the shiny mahogany. The bandmaster is invited to have a glass of port by the president of the mess. The band leader seats himself, and sips his wine. Follows then the toast to the King.

At the mess of the largest Royal Naval Air Station in England they have, by good fortune, obtained the services of a chef who formerly was of the Ritz Hotel in London; and especial attention is given to this mess. No matter how hard may have been the day's work or how many men have been forced to leave for other billets, the dinners there are a sight for the gods. More than 150 expert seaplane pilots from all over the world sit down.

It is like a bit of history of olden days to hear: "Gentlemen, 'The King,'" with its charm and ceremony.

VIII. THE ROYAL NAVAL AMBULANCE TRAIN

READY to speed to any accessible port on telegraphic or telephonic orders from the Admiralty Medical Transport Department are Royal Naval Ambulance trains. They are always on the move, picking up wounded or sick officers and bluejackets at Scotch and English ports, bearing them to stations where there are great hospitals, to relieve the coast institutions likely to receive wounded in the event of a North Sea Fleet engagement. These grey-painted trains, with the Red Cross and the "R.N." on each coach, are the outcome of a great deal of study, and they are now run with remarkable efficiency. No millionaire could receive better care when wounded or ill than do John Bull's naval officers and seamen.

Sir James Porter, the head of this service, whose pen sends a train to all parts of England and Scotland, has a loyal staff, which devotes remarkable zeal to their share of the work. They take pride in making a time-record in disembarkation and entraining of patients. Naval surgeons at each railroad station watch the work of the stretcher-bearers to be sure that every cot has the gentlest possible handling when being carried from the train to the ambulance which is to take the patient to the local hospital.

The "stepping" of the stretcher-bearers seems a trifling thing, but it is surprising to note the attention given to this point in the first days of the war. Dr. A. V. Elder, staff surgeon of the Royal Naval Volunteer Reserve and the right bower of Sir James Porter, practised for weeks the carrying of patients, getting into cots to ascertain the most comfortable step for the wounded. Prizes were even given to the men who carried a pail of water on a cot and reached a fixed point with the most liquid in the receptacle. By this means the best method of "stepping off" was evolved. There are hundreds of these stretcher-bearers—volunteers without compensation—who now perform the task so well that it attracts even the attention of the casual observer. The cot-bearers are doing their "bit"; they get to the railroad stations at all times to meet the ambulance trains, and often have to wait hours and give up their usual business.

It may also be interesting to some that in those August days the Naval Ambulance trains were not much more than a series of box-cars. The present cot—an ingenious arrangement by naval surgeons—was used in the naval hospitals and aboard the warships. But the fixtures on the train for carrying this cot were far from perfection. The patient was tossed about by the movement of the train, and it was realised that in the event of hundreds of patients being carried something would have to be discovered to steady the beds. Dr. Elder invented a clip-spring to be attached to the cot and the side of the coach. It held the bed, and had sufficient "give" to make it steady. In lieu of the box-cars, there are now coaches of the American type, with windows and great sliding doors which permit of easy ingress or egress.

The railroad officials have listened to the bidding of the Medical Transport Officer of the Admiralty and have attached some of the best locomotives to these trains, usually of twelve coaches. Even when there has not been an action, and the trains are bearing mostly medical cases, all passenger and freight traffic gives way to the ambulance trains. If the surgeon in charge of the train decides that he has a case which should be hastened to a hospital he wires ahead, so that when he reaches that point the surgeon or the agent there is on hand with an ambulance to rush the patient to a local hospital.

Where it is possible, red tape has been eliminated. The cots in which the patients are carried are sent with the patient from a hospital or ship, and the patient is only taken out when he arrives at the hospital of his destination. For the cot bearing the patient, the train surgeon receives in exchange a clean cot. This cot has been laundered and fumigated, and is kept on the train so that when only patients are entrained the surgeon gives a cot for each case taken aboard. Hence the surgeon always has the same number of cots on his train, and through this means paper and pencil work is avoided. The patient's clothes are packed in a bag, and all the valuables of one batch of patients are sealed up in one envelope, which is receipted for by the surgeon of the hospital to which the patients are sent.

No patient is transferred from a hospital in a critical condition if it can be avoided. But sometimes this is necessary, as it was following the Jutland Battle. Then the most serious cases were held in the hospitals; while, where it was possible, hundreds of cases were despatched to institutions at other ports.

The route of these ambulance trains may differ every round trip. One ambulance train may go to the North of Scotland, while the next one will only go to Glasgow or Edinburgh if there is no call further north. The wonderful organisation not only undertakes to relieve hospitals, but also to ship the patients to institutions unlikely to be suddenly burdened with many cases; and consideration is also given as to where the patient can receive the best attention, such as in southern hospitals.

Fleet-Surgeon A. Stanley Nance is the Medical Transport Officer for Scotland. He is ever on the alert for what is going on in the hospitals in his territory. In the event of a great sea conflict, he receives orders from Sir James Porter and information concerning all the trains which are by that time racing to the ports nearest to the scene of the engagement.

In London, the Medical Transport Officer can place his finger on a railroad map at any time and tell within a mile or so where his trains are. If by any possible chance they are delayed he receives word from the train surgeons.

Knowing the probability of further engagements in the North Sea, quite a number of wealthy private individuals have interested themselves in the hospitals on the East Coast from north to south. And these persons take especial interest in the trains, many of them making it a point to be at the railroad station whenever a Royal Naval Ambulance train pulls in. What with sick men and accidents, the trains now and again may have a full quota of patients without there having been a fleet engagement. In war time no man who is not physically fit is kept aboard ship, for he may not take up another man's place without being able to perform his work.

Exigencies of war have caused the speedy transformation of buildings in many parts of England into hospitals. There also are institutions constructed in temporary form, architecturally not works of art, but wonderfully useful. The surgeons at these latter places have wrought marvels in obtaining good light in the wards and operating-rooms, and creating a comfortable atmosphere in the exteriorly dingy places.

The starting-point or headquarters of the ambulance trains is in the South, and when they plough their way North they carry no patients. The complement of these trains is from forty to fifty hands, and they all look upon the train as a ship, and use sailors' terms. It is the "Sick Bay Express."

IX. A RUN IN A ROYAL NAVAL AMBULANCE TRAIN

I OBTAINED permission to make a "voyage" in an ambulance train.

On a grey, drizzling morning one of the Royal Naval trains glided into a siding at Queensferry—a dozen miles from Edinburgh. In less than ten minutes six hefty stretcher-bearers steadily and silently bore the first cot patient from a waiting ambulance to the war-coloured train. Cot then followed cot with precision, only two of the patients being in the open at a time; and as quickly as mortals could accomplish it these cots were set swinging in the "eyes" set for the lanyards.

Being about half-past eight o'clock, nobody had much to say. The faces of the sick and wounded bluejackets told you nothing as they lazily gazed around them while being hoisted into the hospital train. They looked like men sewed into white sailcloth sacks. Surgeons, with two and three gold stripes, between which runs the red—blood red, some say—denoting their department in the Navy, glanced occasionally at the patients.

"Carry on, there," then came from the R.N.V.R. lieutenant in charge of the stretcher-bearers, when one of the coaches had received its quota of sick and wounded. Then the sliding doors of the next coach yawned for its measure of sick men, who presented an interesting rather than a pathetic picture, for every bluejacket wore his cap, looking like a sailor who had gone to bed with his clothes on. That cap travels with him like his papers. The bluejacket has many important things which he conceals in it, and the most important of all is his package of "gaspers," as he terms his particular brand of cigarettes. The cap is placed firmly on his head, and occasionally a flannelled arm protruded from the cot. No moan or groan escaped from these plucky patients, for the sailor always lives up to the traditions of the Royal Navy.

From one of the cots there showed a head covered in bandages with only two small openings for the patient's eyes. His cap was on his bed. As this sailor was being hoisted into the train a deep voice came from the bed:—

"Mind yer eye, Bill, or yer'll get yer feet wet."

Bill was a "sitting case." He had come up on the same ambulance as his pal. He had been in the same fo'castle and had been hurt in the same accident. And now they were going aboard the same train to the same port. Bill paid little heed at that moment to his chum as he picked his way through the water and mud. His right arm was in a sling and the comforting cigarette between his teeth. Standing on the last rung of the little ladder before going into the car, I heard him say to another sailor:—

"She's over yonder. Bye-bye for the present."

His cap came off as he looked in the direction of the great deep water where lay the hazy forms of ships. Others looked, but said nothing about the sailor doffing his cap to his grey-steel sweetheart who had weathered the fight against odds.

"That makes 110," said the train surgeon. "Six, four, seventy-three, twenty-seven—what?"

The first two numerals denote officers, sitting and cot cases, and the latter two those of the men.

"Right-o," quoth the officer of the stretcher-bearers.

Soon the grey train steamed out, with orders to make a stop for a couple of cot cases in Edinburgh. In the Waverley Station a few minutes later the train took aboard the patients, and then sped on south.

Before "she" had been under way very long, the surgeon in charge and his assistant walked through the coaches, observing the cases on board and noting whether any of them needed any special attention.

At noon the cooks and stewards were hustling, giving food to men who, I supposed, would only require toast and beef-tea. But it takes a lot to make a bluejacket lose his hunger.

"They're all 'Oliver Twists,'" declared the train surgeon.

Now, there is nothing that a sailor of His Majesty's Navy likes so much to look at as a pretty girl. Hence it was not surprising when I heard a voice from one of the cots, after the train had stopped at Newcastle, in enthusiastic tones blurt out:—

"From 'ere I can see the purtiest gal I ever laid eyes on."

Business, then, of a movement in every cot. Eyes were all front, gazing in the direction of a golden-haired beauty, who blushed a deep pink when she realised how many pairs of eyes from the train were focussed on her. Soon horny hands were being kissed in her direction. Shyly, she sent a kiss or two back, and then retired to the shadows.

As I said before, the train is considered a ship. It is a case of going to "Sick Bay" and of "out pipes" at nine o'clock. They talk of "darkening the ship" when the blinds are pulled and the lights covered. We arrived at Hull when it was dusk, and at the station was, among other persons, Lady Nunburnholme, whose husband is the chief owner of the Wilson Line of steamships, and who takes a deep interest in the ambulance trains and the sailors' hospital in her town. No matter at what hour one of the Royal Naval trains is due, Lady Nunburnholme is at the depot, always eager to have a word with the men, and give them cigarettes and cheer them up.

By error, that evening a clergyman or naval chaplain, who had been hurt on a warship, was put in the coach with the men. The surgeon made the discovery, and said he would have the padre moved into the officers' quarters at the next stop.

"I'm a humbug," said the cheery pastor. "There's nothing wrong with me. Just go ahead looking after the men."

Plymouth was to be the next stop. We were due there at half-past seven o'clock the following morning. At midnight the chief surgeon walked through the train to see that all was well, and he was attracted by a man coughing. He directed that something be given to this patient.

"Don't want to have one man keep half a dozen awake needlessly," said the surgeon.

Then there was an officer who could not go to sleep. He was a medical case, suffering from rheumatism. But what kept him awake was the thought that he might lose his ship. There was a sailor who had fallen on his vessel, knocked four of his teeth out, and cut his head. Why he had to go to "Sick Bay" for such a trifle was beyond him. In the dark hours of the early morning one might have seen the faithful surgeon again going through his train, speaking in whispers to those who lay awake, asking them if there was anything they needed and what pain they had.

"I've got pains all over me, and me 'ead feels scorchin' with the bangin' that's goin' on inside," said one man.

"That's a grumble to get a drink," said the surgeon, who told the man to try to go to sleep.

Devonshire was the scene of gladsome sunshine when the train steamed into the station, delivered certain patients, and picked up others for another port. In his anxiety to get a truck out of the way to permit the stretcher-bearers uninterrupted passage to the ambulances, a porter tipped over six and a half dollars' worth of milk. The patients grinned at this, and the Surgeon-General on the platform appeared to be sorry that so much good milk had gone to waste.

The terminus of the train was reached at half-past seven in the evening. There the coaches were cleared of all patients and the train split in two to permit of traffic passing. The train-surgeon, having delivered the valuables of the patients, walked with me to the naval barracks, where for the first time in thirty-six hours he had a chance to really rest.

"Chin-chin," said he, lifting his glass. "Another run over, and the Germans have not come out yet for the real fight."

X. A TRIP IN A SUBMARINE

THE man who craves excitement is apt to get his fill for a while after a trip in a British submarine under the North Sea. He may dream of the experience for many nights afterwards, and the lip of the conning-tower well seems to get higher and higher until the water rushes over like an incipient Niagara—then he awakens.

The wind was blowing about 30 knots when I boarded the mother ship of the submarines in the English East Coast port. It was an unsettled sort of morning, and just after I had walked over two narrow planks to the under-sea craft, aboard which I was to make a cruise under the North Sea, the sun shot forth a widening streak of blurred silver like a searchlight on the prancing green-grey waves. With care, the two-striper skipper gave his orders to get the submarine under way, and soon he stuck her nose at the east. One felt the frost in the air, and fingers grasping the canvas shield of the conning tower were benumbed.

Three men stood in line on the aft hatch while the submersible glided through the port waters. Four other sailors were getting a last good lungful of fine fresh sea air for'd. At the conning tower were the commander, his helmsman, and a young lieutenant—the boss of the torpedoes. Now and again another officer popped up his head through the conning-tower well, and that opening to the boat's bowels appeared just about large enough for his broad shoulders. The nose of the shark-like craft passed through white-caps as steadily as a ship on a calm ocean.

"Hands for'd, sir," announced the junior lieutenant.

The commander mumbled an answer, and the men were ordered to close the for'd hatches, and soon the iron doors were screwed down. The gas engines shot off black smoke into the curdling wake of the vessel's twin propellers, and as we surged along into the uninteresting sea the skipper sang out to have the aft hatches shut. The well-disciplined bluejackets instantly obeyed the order, and the iron slabs banged to, and I knew that those men were busying themselves in their particular work of seeing that everything was ready for submerging.

The commander of the submarine was an agile man, about 5 feet 7 inches tall. His face looked tired, and there were lines about his eyes, which were only for his ship. I do not think that he had the chance to give me a look— a real look—all the time I was aboard. There was always something which needed his attention. I found that the speed we were making against the wind closed my eyes, for there is very little protection on the conning tower of a submarine; and that alone might have given the commander that tired look. But I gathered afterwards that the eyes are strained a good deal in looking for enemy craft. There, in the distance, was the port whence we had emerged, and we now were out on the breast of the sea in war time. Two miles off our port bow was a grey vessel, to which our skipper gave his attention for a while. She was a British destroyer plunging through the water at 22 knots.

The sun had disappeared behind a bank of clouds, but there were still streaks of blue in the sky. The commander shot his gaze aft, to starboard, port, and before him. Although we were heading straight out to sea, the skipper was ever on the alert.

"Motors ready?" asked the commander of the sub-lieutenant, whose head showed up from the well after communicating with the engine-room chief artificer.

"Motors ready, sir," was the answer, and the younger man wrung his cold hands.

By that time England's coast was a hazy outline. But on we cut through the waves until England disappeared, and soon after the real thrill came—the thrill of going down under an angry ocean. The gas engines were stopped, and the way on the craft was allowed to carry her a good distance, following the order from the commander.

That officer looked around, and signalled to a British destroyer—another of the warships ploughing the waters of the North Sea. A sailor expert signalman used his arms as semaphores, and an answer soon was received by our skipper.

On the engine-room telegraph of the submarine is a word that does not figure on the apparatus of other types of warships: it is "Dive." The commander told me that we were going down very soon. I observed that the destroyer had turned around and was heading out to sea. We were almost at a stop, when our skipper told me to get into the conning-tower well and to be down far enough to give him room. It must be realised that immediately after the order to submerge has been rung in the engine-room the conning-tower hatch is closed. Hence the commander and his helmsman have no time to lose when the submarine is going under, as it takes forty-five seconds to submerge an under-sea craft, and at times, if pressed, it can be accomplished in thirty seconds.

Up to that time I had not devoted much attention to the inside of the conning-tower hatch, beyond glancing at the brass ladder. Soon I discovered that there were two ladders, and that the distance to the inside deck of the boat was about twice as great as I had imagined.

After I had taken my foot off the last rung of the ladder and stepped on the chilled, wet canvas-covered iron deck, my head was in a whirl at the sight of the bowels of brass and steel. The skipper had set the arrow at "Dive," and we were going down and down—a motion which is hardly perceptible to the layman.

The activity below and the intricate mechanism of the craft caused me to think more of what the men were doing than of my own sensations. I wondered how one man could learn it all, for the skipper must have an intimate knowledge of all the complicated machinery of his vessel. There were engines everywhere and little standing room—at least, that is how it appeared on the first glance, and even afterwards it was clear that no adipose person could hope to survive aboard a submarine.

No sooner had the engine-room received the order to submerge than the captain followed his helmsman down the conning-tower hatch, and he lost not a second in getting to the periscope—the eye of his vessel. Soon my attention was arrested by the sight of two men sitting side by side turning two large wheels. One kept his eye on a bubble and turned his wheel to control the hydroplanes to keep the craft level, and the other man's eyes also watched a bubble in a level. His share of the work was to keep the vessel at the depth ordered by the commander.

Although I was deeply interested in everything that went on under the sea in that craft, my eyes were continually on the captain, who looked like a photographer about to take the picture of a wilful baby. The skipper's face was concealed behind two black canvas wings of the reflector, which keep the many electric lights aboard from interfering with his view through the glass. I then noticed a door in the stern of the craft—about amid-ships—a door which is closed on the sight of danger. To me it looked like a reflection, but you soon find out that you are looking at the engines of the submarine. There, four or five men, ignoring whether they were under the water or on the surface, were concentrated on their work. One mistake, and the submarine and its crew are lost. Hence there is no inattention to duty. Finally, this door was slammed to.

The air below is not much different to what it is when the vessel is on the surface—or not noticeably different until the craft has been submerged for several hours. It is then that the "bottles" or air tanks are brought into play. I walked to the bows of the boat, where a giant torpedo was greased and ready for the shutting of its compartment. The air-tight tube was then locked down, and the missile was ready for its victim. But, as I said, lured as you may be to gaze at the other parts of the wonderful craft, you will find that your gaze comes back to the captain—always at the periscope, hands on those brass bars that turn the periscope, and eyes glued to the reflector.

"Lower periscope!" he orders. And then: "Raise periscope!" He gives these orders with clearness; not surprising, as no command must be misunderstood when you are 25 or 30 feet under the water.

"Lower periscope!"

A man in a corner, next to one who has charge of the gyroscopic compass, turns a handle, and the greased steel cylinder sinks until the captain, who had been stretched with toes tipped, now is on bended knees, his hands extended to stop the periscope man from taking the "eye" further down. The captain turns the periscope around, scanning the waters. At his right, when the skipper is facing the bows, is another officer, with his hand on the trigger of what looks like an upward-pointed pistol of brass and steel. This officer waits for the command to send off the torpedo.

"Lower foremost periscope into the well," ordered the captain. This periscope was not in use and had not been above the surface. It is the duplicate "eye," in case the other is out of order.

"Yes," said the captain, not looking at me, "she's mostly guts below. Have a look at that destroyer. We are going to send a practice torpedo at her, and she will pick it up and return it when we get back home."

The sleek, lean warship was knifing the waters at 22 knots. It was like looking at a picture—a moving picture—and all was beautifully distinct. Our commander consulted a card, decided the speed of the warship, and then again propped his head against the reflector.

"Raise periscope," ordered the two-striper.

For the first time aboard the submarine, there was something akin to silence, except for the swishing of engines and the continuous buzz of other mechanism.

"Light to starboard," voiced the captain.

"Light to starboard," repeated the helmsman at the compass.

"Tube ready?" asked the commander, his head hidden between the black flaps of the periscope.

"Tube ready, sir."

The officer at the trigger stood like a starter at a race, his finger on the tongue that was to release the torpedo. It was just as it is in the real moment of moments and a war craft is the target. The men at the two wheels watched their dials and their bubbles, and the helmsman had his nose on the needle. The commander, the gold braid on his cuffs streaked with oil and rust, then had but one thought in his mind—to hit the target.

He looked neither to right nor left but was still at the periscope. The warship was there. We were there, and one could imagine the tiny periscope just above the water. The situation was tense, even if the vessel to be fired at was not an enemy craft.

"Fire!" snapped the captain.

It was no order for men to spring "over the top," no battle-cry that was heard by the enemy, but the word under the water that is the order for the deadly destroyer to be released and speed on its way to the unsuspecting craft. Practice torpedo or not, when under the waves of the North Sea the word works up a dramatic situation hard to equal. The other officers and men are interested, and they told me that never does the word "Fire" fail to stir the soul of everybody aboard. Though the effect is heightened by the knowledge that a great vessel is the target and has been bored in twain, the interest is still thrilling when the submarine is practising. With a shot at the enemy there is, of course, the explosion to dread. If the submarine does not get away far enough, the explosion of the torpedo may be the cause of extinguishing all lights aboard the submarine, and lamps have then to be used.

There was a tiger-like growl or "g-r-rh" of anger as the tube sent out the greased steel complicated missile, and outside I pictured the white wake that streaked in the direction of the warship. It was not visible from the periscope, which a second after the signal to fire had been brought down under the surface. The comparative stillness was gone, and the inside of the submarine seemed to have awakened from a doze. There was all bustle and hurry around me. The captain shot a look at the gyroscopic compass and gave orders for the motors to go ahead, and for half an hour the submarine pushed about under the surface. Then the commander had the periscope raised, and on the distant horizon I made out the destroyer—a tiny thing even in the glass of the magnifying lens of the under-sea boat's "eye."

My feet were numbed with cold as I walked for'd and looked at the empty tube. These torpedoes cost £500 (two thousand, five hundred dollars), and in war time they are all set to sink if they fail to hit the target; set to sink because they might be used by the enemy or get in our own way.

The next thrilling moment came when the commander decided to bring his craft to the surface.

"Come to surface and blow external tanks!" ordered the two-striper. "Open five, six, seven, eight, to blow!"

The round, white perforated lungs of the submarine sucked in the air in the craft.

"Open one, two, three, four, to blow," came from the skipper.

"One, two, three, four, to blow," I heard repeated.

I felt no perceptible motion of ascending; but those lungs were working hard, which could be learned by placing your hand over them. The captain shot a glance at the dial, which told him how far up his vessel had gone, and then mounted the conning-hatch ladder, and soon one observed a spot of daylight. A sea washed over the submarine, filling the commander's boots with water. He was followed by a sailor, who quickly attached the lowered sailcloth bridge to the rails of the conning tower. Then the captain's expert and watchful eye caught bubbles coming from one of the tanks.

"Close one!" he shouted down the hatch.

"Close one," repeated the sub-lieutenant.

"Two, five, and seven," came from the voice outside, and so on, until soon all the tanks had pumped out their water and were filled with air; and, for the sake of accuracy, each order was sounded again below.

"Bring her around to north," said the commander.

When we submerged it had been a chilly day, with a peep of the sun every now and again. The weather had changed since we left our berth under the sea. The sky was overcast, and snow was falling. And this change in the weather had taken place while the captain had been accomplishing one of Jules Verne's dreams.

We sped farther out to sea; this time on the *qui vive* for enemy craft. But the enemy is careful not to give the British submarine much of a chance at his warships, only sneaking out occasionally under cover of darkness with a couple of destroyers. Nevertheless, John Bull's diving boats are ever on the alert; and the man with whom I went under the North Sea had performed deeds of daring which never involved the sinking of a neutral vessel or of endangering the life of a non-belligerent.

It was the time for luncheon. Luncheon! You get an idea that the life aboard a submarine is not all sunshine and white uniforms when you see the berth for the commander and his chief officer. They are just a couple of shelves, and are not used very often at that. It was explained to me that when you are running a submarine you do not go in much for sleep. Luncheon consisted of a cup of coffee and a piece of canned beef on a stale slice of bread. Tinned food is about all that can be used aboard a submarine. It does not take up much room, and it requires little in the way of cooking utensils. We were still having our luncheon below when we dived again, so for the first time in my life I found myself having a meal under the sea.

It was hours afterwards that we slipped into the darkened harbour and found the mother ship, where the officers enjoy some of the real comforts of life.

"Have a Pandora cocktail?" asked my captain.

We imbibed joyfully. The commander then changed his clothes, and we sat down to dinner—a late dinner, most of the other members of the mess having finished half an hour before.

And if you ask me about sensations while under the water, again I must confess that I was too busy looking and learning to experience anything but a fear that I might omit something of importance during the time the captain was getting ready for his target. Being under the sea, however, gave me a thrill felt long afterwards, and I left knowing something of the hardships that England's sea dogs suffer while guarding their island kingdom.

XI. LIFE IN A LIGHTHOUSE

THE old man led the way to the sturdy stone structure on top of which were the great horns which sound the warning in foggy weather to ships at sea. He was proud of the lighthouse, of which he was the principal keeper; and just before he started to explain to me the wonders of the compressed-air engines, he remarked:—

"First, you must know that a lighthouse-keeper's job is to watch for a fog."

"What's your name?" I asked. He was the first real lighthouse-keeper I had met.

The lighthouseman looked at me and then at one of the coast-watchers. He was a slender man of about sixty years, who, I had been told, was enjoying the work he had set out to do long, long before there was a thought of a great war.

"T. G. Cutting," he replied, "the P.K. here."

It was on the western Cornish coast, where, as in other places in and off English shores, the lighthouses, war or no war, from sunset to sunrise cut the darkness with their long beams of whiteness and, when necessary, sound the foghorn. You do not see any young men who are not in khaki or navy blue, and the old men are wonders, with their binoculars and telescopes. Mr. Cutting had been within sound of the sea ever since he was born. First, he had seen service on a lighthouse on the rocks, as they say, and from the rocks he graduated to a land job, and thence back to the rocks, and again on to the land. We read stories of the lighthouse-keeper; but little is written on the modern man of this species. Mr. Cutting is not accustomed to the glare of the city's lights, but he knows the glare of a lighthouse-lantern and all the various wonders of the work.

Inside the annex to the lighthouse were the duplicate engines for filling tanks with compressed air. This air is used for blowing the foghorns, and when they sound everybody in the locality knows it.

"Enough air is stored in those tanks," declared Mr. Cutting, "to keep the foghorns going for twenty minutes. That gives us time to get the engines running."

He went into details of the engines, showing that he knew them by heart, and I could almost imagine the blurring, deafening sound which for seven seconds rent the air through the roar of winds every minute and a half.

"Fog, as you know, is the dread of every sea captain," said Mr. Cutting. "Out yonder you see the 'Three Stone Orr Rocks.' This is a dangerous bit of scenery in foggy weather. When we have a fog, two men are on duty; one if it is clear."

We then went to the lighthouse tower, which stands nearly 200 feet above high water. To the right, on entering that building, was a blacksmith's shop, with an anvil, forge, and various implements. This forge is occasionally needed to make repairs, spare parts, and accessories of the engines of the lighthouse. To the right, in a corridor, were speaking-tubes.

"Those tubes go to the bedside of every man employed here," said Mr. Cutting. "We have only to blow, and in a few minutes he comes up to the lighthouse. Our houses are over there, in the same structure as the tower. They are practically the lower portion of the main building."

He conducted the way up the narrow, winding stairs. At the head of the first flight I saw a green-covered book, in which every man on watch makes his entry of the weather, the velocity of the wind, and so forth.

"Many a man's word has been corrected by that book," said the P.K. "And here's the book for privileged visitors, for nobody comes here without the proper credentials."

There were names of famous persons inscribed in the book, which was kept as neatly and cleanly as everything else in the place.

"Now we'll go up to the lantern," said the old man. Old, but lithe, strong, and keen-eyed. He is particularly fond of this lantern, and was remarkably lucid in explaining everything concerning the working of it.

"Does the sea ever come up as high as this?" I asked.

"We get the spray, and that is all," answered the P.K. "It's dirty weather when that happens. But the water usually has spent its force when it reaches this height."

The exterior windows of the lantern were diamond shaped and of plate glass. In the middle of the lantern was the large concentric-ringed glass of great magnifying power.

"You can turn it round with your little finger," said the P.K. "That's because it floats in a mercury bath. And in turning that you are moving four tons. When the lantern is lighted, it shows dark for seven and a half seconds, then two sets of four flashes, making a complete revolution every half-minute. They can see the light at sea on a clear night for nineteen miles. The light is worked by vaporised oil. The compressed air drives the oil to the lantern, up through that burner in a hole hardly big enough to take a pin point. It is nearly half a million candle-power. This type of light is considered even better than electricity. In the old-style oil-lights they burned five quarts in the same time that this one consumes a pint with better results."

The actual burner of the lantern is disappointing, as one expects to see a giant burner. Really, it is only about twice the size of the average household one.

Mr. Cutting observed that the light was carefully timed, and called attention to the half-minute hand on the clock in the tower. Persons are always asking the P.K. how he spends his time, and he wondered why. He believed that anybody ought to see that there was plenty for a man to do while he is on a four hours' watch in the tower. The turning of the light, showing black outside and then flashing its warnings, after his many years of experience of such things, is only taken for granted by this P.K.

"And when I've finished lighting the lamp, trimming up things a bit," said the P.K., "I sit down like anybody else. Lots of people seem to forget that the lighthouse-keeper is not the coast-guard or the head of the crew of a life-saving station. They have their work to attend to, but we watch for fogs night and day. When a man is stationed at a lighthouse like the Longships, which is a little distance out on a rock, he may be a couple of months without being relieved. But he has others with him, and a good stock of food. If he wishes to communicate with the land, he does so by signals; and that's the way men over there talk with their wives who live in cottages on shore. The telephone has not been found feasible, wires breaking all the time; so their wives have learned to wig-wag to them.

"One night they got a scare on shore; thought that the men on the Longships were sending up distress signals. It was bad weather, and every now and again the coast-watcher saw a green light on the Longships. And what do you think that green light was? Just the water running over the bright light when it flashed! As it washed the glasses it showed up green."

There were curtains of sailcloth put over the windows to obscure the sunlight. I asked the P.K. about this, and he told me that the great magnifying lens of the light would burn things if the sun got on it for long enough. So, much as they like the sun in Cornwall, they have to keep it out.

"I shall be on duty to-night from twelve until four o'clock," observed the P.K. "But I've got accustomed to the running of the machinery."

So down we went. The last I saw of the P.K. was when the old Cornishman, emptying cans of oil into the tank to supply the light which warns mariners, shouted:—

"Getting pretty fresh now. Hope to see you again."

XII. WATCHERS OF THE COAST

CIRCLING Great Britain are thousands of expert coast-watchers, whose duty not only is to watch for ships, wrecks, and smugglers, as in the days before the war, but also to be on guard for enemy submarines and suspicious craft. It is the oft-spoken opinion of many an inland inhabitant that certain sections of the coast would afford a base for U-boats. However, these persons have no conception of the thoroughness with which John Bull guards his coast-lines. Mile after mile, shores and rocks are under the eye of alert navy men and volunteers, the latter being civilians who have spent their lives by the sea. They know their business, and even though they are volunteers, the discipline is rigid. But they are not the type of men to shirk their duty, for they would take it as missing a God-given opportunity if their eyes were closed at the time they could help their country most. After travelling around part of the coast-line, a stranger leaves with the opinion that there is little chance for a man even to swim ashore under cover of night.

From John o' Groat's to Land's End and all around Ireland, these coast-watchers—men over military age, wiry and strong, with eyes like ferrets—scan the rocks and beaches hour after hour, noting passing vessels, receiving and detailing information, and always keeping up communication with the ring and its various centres. Their little stone huts are on the highest point in their particular area, and their homes usually are only a couple of hundred yards distant. Their chiefs are coast-guards of the old days called back to their former service in the Royal Navy. These men rule the volunteers with a rod of iron. No matter what section of the coast one may pick, the coast-watcher is ready with his glasses or telescope. Suspicious acts of any individuals receive speedy attention, and each batch of the guards vies with the next for keen performance of duty.

There is a halo of interest around these men, tame as their work may appear to them at times. Take the watchers on the Scilly Isles, for instance. They are as good as any around Great Britain. It is second nature for them to watch the sea. It is a desire with them, something they would not miss. Their fathers, grandfathers, and great-grandfathers were watch-dogs on that area of the ocean. Go to St. Mary's, and you will see a coast-watcher, up soon after dawn, take a stroll along the beach, even when he is not supposed to be on duty and before he has tasted his morning tea. The family telescope is at his eye, as he wants to get a good look at what the sea has been doing, and what is there. To the uninitiated, it seems to have the same paucity of interest as any other shipless stretch of water; but to this expert it has a story. He notes the clouds, the sun, the very rocks; and they say that his gaze is so sharp that it would spot a champagne-cork floating some distance away. But be that as it may, there is no enemy periscope that is going to pass unobserved at a certain distance by this hawk-eyed, wind-seared man.

He goes to his cottage for breakfast, and talks about the sea, then leaves the table, and has another good look; and it is sadly disappointing to any of these men to have missed a passing ship. Prior to the declaration of hostilities, a wreck was the greatest piece of news to the community; but now it is the glimpse of fast English warships, and the anticipation of sighting a German U-boat, and thus being the cause of the craft's doom.

"Gun-firing heard at ten minutes past twelve o'clock to-day," said one man, reading from a slip he had just made out on the subject.

The man to whom he spoke happened to have been out of hearing distance, and he could not believe it until a second man came along with the same report. It was handed down the line, over to other shores, and the watchers speculated as to what had taken place.

Arthur Oddy, who has charge of half a dozen watchers, told me that his one great regret was that he had not seen a sign of the war, barring uniforms. Nevertheless, for more than two and a half years he has scanned the sea and shore of his district with dutiful care, and has seen to it that his men have not been amiss in their share of the tedious task. His station is very near the Last House in England, at Land's End—a tea place kept by Mrs. E. James.

"What is that out there?" exclaimed a stranger, suddenly. "Looks like part of a boat."

"That," declared Oddy, "is the Shark's Fin—a rock."

True enough, the rock of that name might have at times been a giant fish or a wrecked submarine. It was lashed by the foamy waters, disappeared, and then showed a bit, again was swallowed up, and seemed to reappear a yard or so further along from where it first was seen. Finally, you observed that it was a sharp, dangerous rock.

A mile or so farther along that coast I encountered John Thomas Wheeler, the wearer of several medals, including a gold one received since the war commenced from the King of Sweden. In peace time, just before the war, Wheeler did his bit to save wrecked mariners. He is still doing it in war time, with his eyes open for everything. As we stood there, with the sea lashing the shingly beach and hammering the rocks, Wheeler, chief officer of that station, recalled the story of the wreck of the *Trifolium*, a Swedish sailing ship.

"It was terrible rough," said Wheeler, "when through the darkness we saw the green light of the distress-signals. I shot off a rocket with a rope to the forepart of the vessel. The men, who were clinging to the rigging, paid no attention to it. Then I sent off another rope between the main and the mizzen masts. First, they paid no heed to that; but, finally, one man in oilskins jumped into the sea to catch hold of part of the rope. He was followed by others. Perilous though it was on that night, we walked out to help the men ashore. One after another, gasping and unconscious sailors were landed. Then the ship broke in half, and soon was torn to bits by the sea. I was looking for more men, as I had seen one poor chap under the steel mast when it fell. A wave struck me, and I found myself caught between two rocks. It looked all up for me, as I could not move."

Wheeler's awful position was not at first realised, and his cries for help could not be heard through the din of the ocean. Finally, he was struck down by the turbulent sea, and one of his men, signalling to another, went to their chief's rescue. Wheeler was unconscious when he was brought up on the beach. For his share in the rescue work, besides the King of Sweden's medal, Wheeler received medals from the Royal Humane Society and the Board of Trade.

In that corner of England every one is on the *qui vive* for the unexpected. The women have their telescopes and glasses, and they do their share, despite the fact that the regular men of that locality are on duty. Mrs. James's tea-refreshment place is often the near-by house to where men are scanning the horizon with their glasses, noting the flags on vessels, if they have any in these days, and keeping up a peace-time look out, for it is a dangerous point in bad weather. The Last or First House in England, whichever one wishes to consider it, is covered with names and initials of persons from all over the world. Curiously enough, since the war there have been no wrecks in that theatre, while in the six months prior to the great conflict there were two or three.

Local heads of the coast-watchers or guards have the prerogative of commandeering horses or automobiles when necessary. If there is a ship ashore or on the rocks, signal-rockets are sent up to collect the coast-guards; and it would seem that a couple of these would wake most of the persons in that corner of England.

The real business of the coast-guards, and that to which they devote themselves in peace or war, is firing rockets over a ship in distress and trying to land the crew.

It was ten or twelve miles from that point that I met a chief watcher who had been blown up in a British battleship, and had thus earned a period of shore duty. He was "carrying on" for humanity and country, and only a short time before he had been the means of rescuing the crew of a small neutral sailing ship—a German victim.

We sped on farther north, and every three or four miles there was the inevitable watcher, who can telephone, telegraph, and fire rockets when occasion demands. It is all a modernised coast-guard system, the men being first ready for ships in distress, but always on the alert for the enemy.

XIII. CROSSING THE CHANNEL IN WAR TIME

THIS is the story of a British naval officer's trip to the Western fighting ground as he told it to me the day he returned to London:—

"'Four days!' said I to myself. 'Not very long in which to get a real taste of the World War on land.' However, the morning after I had received 'leave' I departed from London in an automobile and as we sped through the country there seemed, at first, to be little to remind us that England was at war—except, perhaps, the many busy persons on all farms and fields. Finally, we came across a mobile air-station on which were two aeroplanes with folded wings. It was something which made you think.

"In a South Coast port, however, there was military activity everywhere. On the waters, far out from the harbour, which one imagines as denuded of craft, I saw dozens of ships. There were large and small tramps, mine-sweepers, and trawlers, and you were fascinated by the sight. There was a dread lest one of them might disappear through a mine or a torpedo any instant.

"Thousands of soldiers were at the dock, waiting to embark on ships for France. A couple of thousand of them belonged to the Scotch Labour Battalion, ready for work with pick and shovel. Their speech was almost like a foreign language as they 'Jock'd' and 'Donal'd,' joked and sang, when they swung aboard the vessel in single file.

"There was no waving of handkerchiefs and no shouting good-byes when the black-and-tan craft was ready to leave. The skipper was on the bridge. He looked down at an officer ashore, nodded his head, and the other returned the nod. Hawsers were instantly slipped, and the steamer skipped away from the British port on the minute, and soon met her escort— destroyers, out of sight not long since, now ready for their job. These slender speedsters of the sea never stop; so everything must be done according to schedule. Four of the destroyers surrounded us as we ploughed through the water.

"From the bridge came the order for every soul aboard to put on a life-belt, and our friends from Scotland hastened aft to obtain the equipment, scurrying and bustling about the damp cabin for the best belts.

"Half-way across the straits we met the opposite number vessel to ours. She had an escort of three warships, so that for a flash there were seven destroyers on the breast of that water. But it was not for long. A swish, and they were nearer England and we nearer France, they getting some of our

- 48 -

smoke and we some of theirs. Steamers go into the French port stern first, and soon I found myself treading French soil. Our Scotch labourers were hurried off the vessel, and they vanished with extraordinary quickness; and this also reminds me that no sooner was our steamship safe in the harbour than the warships nipped off to England, and all you could see in a few minutes was a wreath of water and smoke as they raced homewards.

"The skipper of the passenger craft has seen exciting times. While I stood on the bridge with him and his first officer, he told me of a night he won't easily forget. He was running the *Queen*, and going over empty, having smuggled aboard a staff officer who had missed the other vessel. It was darkening, and the *Queen* was about four miles off the British coast when this skipper saw dark hulls, blanched lines, and flaming funnels—all showing terrific speed. First, he took the strange craft to be new French destroyers; but they hailed him in English, and, of course, for an instant he thought then they were British warships, when suddenly it dawned on him. 'By God, they're Germans!' he ejaculated to the staff officer. 'Nip into the cabin, and get those clothes off and into an oilskin, fast as you like.'

"The army man got it done just in time, for an officer and two men from one of the German destroyers sprang aboard the *Queen* after the enemy warship had bumped the passenger craft. The German demanded the captain's papers, and was told that everything had been thrown overboard.

"The Germans were pale, and the pistol in the officer's hand shook dangerously. The skipper declared that the only papers relating to the *Queen* were in his cabin.

"'Get those papers, or I'll blow your head off,' said the German. Below, the captain moved his hand to his hip pocket to get his keys, the German started, and put the muzzle of his revolver close to the Britisher's head. As the captain was unlocking a drawer, the German again became suspicious, and warned the skipper. The Briton told the German to get the papers himself, and, finally, the useless document relating to the *Queen* was taken from the drawer. It was snatched up and pocketed by the German officer. Meanwhile, his men had fixed bombs in vital parts aboard the passenger craft, and the order was given to abandon ship.

"Just before the bang came and the *Queen* sank, the German decided that he wanted to take the skipper with him. Fortunately, the captain had been missed in their tremulous excitement. However, the Germans could not wait, and they had to go away without the skipper. It was an experience no man would forget; and the British of it is that this same man, who had a pretty good chance of spending many months in a German prison camp, is still guiding vessels flying our flag from France to England and England to France.

"In Boulogne, I had to take a train for Paris. It was the longest train I ever set eyes on. One end of it seemed to be in the dock station while the other was on the outskirts of the town. You can get an idea of its length when I say that it had to stop twice at all stations. There was no attempt at speed until we got within twenty miles of Paris."

In a railroad station in Paris this officer encountered a friend who was a commander in the Royal Naval Air Service, and the traveller thereupon decided that nobody could give him a better idea of the war in the brief time at his disposal than this man. Hence, after a dash to the hotel and taking chances of getting his suitcase, the sea-fighter, with only a tooth-brush and a piece of soap, finally joined the flying man, and off they went to the war. My naval friend continued:—

"War stared at us after we had passed through Chantilly, and on the way to Amiens we sped by forty or fifty ambulances. It was at the Café Gobert, in Amiens, that we got out of the automobile and had luncheon. That town was thronged with nonchalant women and blue-clad poilus. Following our refreshment, we continued our journey. We ran into soldiers and guns, aeroplanes, and more guns of all calibres; there must have been two miles of them in one batch that we passed on the way to Arras, as well as 'umpty' parks of lorries.

"The first steam engine that I got a chance of seeing since leaving England was an antiquated London, Chatham, and Dover locomotive attached to a long train of cars filled with provisions and so forth, helped out by Belgian and French engines. The rail-head, not far from that particular 'somewhere,' reminded me of Whiteley's shop in London. Then I observed a dozen fire-engines painted khaki colour. There were officers' baths, coal and wood on lorries, tents, and everything you can think of—and a lot you can't. Ammunition dumps were on our right and left, and the occasional gleam of a sentry's bayonet let you know that somebody was on watch.

"As I was the guest of the Royal Naval Air Service, it was naturally gratifying to come to the home of that service or section of it; the spot which had been barren land two days before was now the scene of great activity. Mess tents were comfortably fixed up, electric light being obtained from lorries. There were workshops on lorries. The Royal Flying Corps also had a station near by. These ingenious Air Service men do all their repairing on the spot. If a lorry gets stuck in the mud they just use enough lorries until they pull it out.

"Our Rolls-Royce darted into the air on one stretch of bad road. It bumped out our dynamo, and we made the rest of the way along the dark road behind a staff car.

"By that time there was no doubt but that we were at the war—passing between two lines of our heavy artillery on the snow covered ground. The splashes of fire—red on the glistening white—formed a memorable picture.

"Every now and again, the snow was lighted up by the star-shells, which hung in the air and then dropped like a rain of gold on the silver ground. The thunder of the guns was pleasing, and as each shell sped on its errand, the unforgettable scene became more beautiful, with the glow from the star-shells and the sight of men, silhouetted in the temporary light against the white-blanketed earth, going about their duty, as some of them had done for more than two and a half years. On we dashed, until we heard a challenging voice, and discerned a French poilu.

"'Aviation anglaise,' announced my friend. After satisfying himself, the sentry permitted us to continue on our way. A little further on, to our chagrin, we learned that a lorry had broken down on a bridge, and that if our car could not pass it, it would mean a detour of nine miles. However, our excellent chauffeur was equal to the occasion. After bending the mud-guards, following the taking of measurements, he drove the machine over in safety with not half an inch to spare.

"Guns boomed as they had been booming for thirty months. This gives you food for thought at the front. Finally, we came to Dunkirk, and there enjoyed uninterrupted repose after our long ride in the biting weather. Next morning I was up early, and before I had breakfast I watched a seaplane turning and twisting, riding first tail downward and then head downward, dropping a thousand feet, and then righting itself, and outdoing the looping-the-loop idea. I ventured commendation for this pilot's exploits.

"'Pretty good youngster,' said the commander. 'Soon be able to give him a journey he's been longing to have.'

"This *youngster* certainly seemed to me a past master in the flying art.

"My interest next was centred on several barges probing their way through the canal. They were manned by soldiers in khaki, and these soldier-sailors belonged to the I.W.T.—the Inland Water Transport.

"Later, I had the satisfaction of firing off one of the big guns at the Huns, and then of going into an observation post from whence we watched shells bursting on the German lines. The Germans were fairly silent, while we were putting over quite a lot of stuff. My next shot at the Boche was with 'Polly,' whose shell spat forth at her opposite number, known on our side of the lines as 'Peanought.'

"It was decidedly interesting in the trenches, almost as near the German lines as we are at any point. There was the occasional thunder of the artillery, coupled with the report of a rifle, which told that the sniper was on the job, and now and again the 'bang-zizz' of the German trench mortar projectile—known better as 'Minnie.'

"At the seaplane station I met a young officer who two days before had flown over from England in the early morning and was to dine that same night with friends in London. His only worry was that he might possibly miss the boat to take him back to keep the dinner engagement. Then there was a young man—eighteen years old, to be specific—who had accounted for thirteen of the enemy aeroplanes.

"My next experience was aboard a destroyer which took me to England. I had not worn an overcoat during my trip, but I was glad of a duffel coat on that speedy craft."

The commander glanced at his watch, and observed he had just half an hour in which to get to King's Cross Station.

Milton Keynes UK
Ingram Content Group UK Ltd.
UKHW011145220424
441551UK00008B/837

9 789357 961453